"To read and meditate upon these delicate, carefully crafted poems is to enter many worlds connected by one life and sustained by a firm and living faith. Their home is Australia – Sydney, the Blue Mountains – but they are of the world from Prague to New Zealand, and the Egypt of the Bible. They live within the happinesses and profound experiences of family and friends. They are to be savoured as they effect the task of all true poetry - to render wonderful again the world in which we live, in its particularities and beauties, its sorrows and its joys, all sustained by the love of God."

> **– David Jasper**, Professor of Literature and Theology, University of Glasgow, Scotland

"In *Trumped by Grace*, Peter Stiles shares a stunning poetic ear. And what is more, since that ear is informed by the Word, we find our joy doubled. He is sensitive to all of life, and so he ranges through a myriad of emotions, situations –creates a pilgrimage of sorts. It's one that will sing you alive again!"

> **– David Craig**, Professor of English, Franciscan University of Steubenville, Ohio

" 'My gaze to the horizon is a prayer,' writes Peter Stiles in one poem. The whole of *Trumped by Grace* is informed by prayer, by attention to what Marilynne Robinson calls the 'difficult, ordinary' life that we live, and by a sense that the things and events we cherish are always in danger of losing their being. The Christian's gaze always seeks to preserve that being, to keep the ordinary in the aura of the sacramental, and that is surely the poetics deeply at work in these poems."

> **– Kevin Hart**, Edwin B Kyle Professor of Christian Studies, University of Virginia.

"Peter Stiles' *Trumped by Grace* is a lyrical triumph. Readers will be moved by his wisdom and wit. Writing in the tradition of George Herbert and Gerard Manley Hopkins, Stiles discerns metaphysical truth in the everyday material world, effortlessly producing poetic pieces that speak of wonder, beauty and truth."

— **Holly Faith Nelson**, Professor and Chair of English, Trinity Western University, Canada

"Here are poems where the writer and reader alike are 'trumped by grace', as the grace of God is caught seeping into an everyday world and transfiguring it. Familiar images from Scripture and Christian belief take on a new life as they are placed in a setting of Australian suburbia, beaches, flora and mountains, where details are sensitively observed and plucked from memory. Music, visual art, conversations and silences are embodied in words which are both sharp-edged and consolatory, sounding the ancient themes of life, death, pain and love in ways that awaken us to a surprising presence here and now. This is a collection which is a considerable achievement both in its expression and in its exploration of a spiritual depth in the cycles of daily experience."

— **Paul S. Fiddes**
Professor of Systematic Theology, University of Oxford.
Principal Emeritus, Regent's Park College, Oxford

TRUMPED BY
grace

PETER STILES

POETICA CHRISTI PRESS

Published by **Poetica Christi Press**
42 Hawkins Rd, Montrose, 3765
Email: poetica@iprimus.com.au
Website: www.poeticachristi.org.au

© 2015, **Peter Stiles**

ISBN: 978-0-9941640-2-5

Cover photograph by **Peter Williams**
Book layout and cover design by **Cameron Semmens**
www.webcameron.com

About
The
Author

Dr. Peter Stiles tutors and lectures at Excelsia College (formerly the Wesley Institute) in Sydney, Australia. He is also an Adjunct Professor of English and Religious Studies at Trinity Western University, Canada, and the inaugural Honorary Research Associate at Morling College, Sydney. In addition he is a visiting lecturer in Australian literature at Houghton College, New York. He completed his Ph.D. in Literature and Theology at the University of Glasgow in 1995. He has published both academic and creative works and his scholarly articles on Elizabeth Gaskell have appeared in journals, conference proceedings, and edited collections. He has experience teaching in both secondary and tertiary settings and has served in the administration of several educational institutions. He is the Australian representative for *Christianity and Literature*, a Fellow of the RSA, a Member of the Australian College of Educators, and a Justice of the Peace (NSW).

Dedication

This collection of verse is dedicated to
my wife, Kerrie;
my children, Rachel (and Andie), Stephen, Andrew (and Hannah);
and my grandchildren Matilda, Jemima, Barnabas, and Gabriel.

Contents

Introduction

Set against the uniquely beautiful but challenging extremes of the Australian and New Zealand landscape, this collection of verse and some prose is representative of my creative concerns over several decades. It reflects, amongst other things, the cycles of my life and my desire to express those experiences within suburban life, on frequent excursions to the pristine beaches near Sydney and during holidays in the stunning Blue Mountains west of this great, harbourside city. Although I have travelled a good deal throughout my life, Australia, more particularly Sydney and surrounding regions, will always be the place where I feel most at home, most at peace.

For northern hemisphere readers a couple of reminders are necessary. As Christmas and Easter are significant, frequently mentioned events on the Christian calendar, it is good to remember that in Australia the festive season is at the height of summer and Easter is during fall. The diminished sense of Christmas being associated with sleigh bells and snow is something that I have lived with all my life, despite the wintery scenes that Christmas cards persist in depicting. Likewise for Easter. It does not come at a time when the natural world reflects rebirth, rather during that month when shorter, cooler days are a foretaste of winter. These reversals to the norm afford a fresh perspective.

Also, the flora and fauna of Australia are very different to the rest of the world. They help to shape our antipodean consciousness in subtle but significant ways. For example, Christmas Bush, a commonly grown but beautiful shrub that is covered in red blossoms throughout December, is often cut in bunches to decorate the home at Christmas time. This is a time, too, when bushfires frequently ravage country areas. Ironically, while they bring destruction to the native forests, they also help other species to germinate. This re-growth is a wondrous scene to witness in the months following such a frightening conflagration. The bird life in Australia is also quite extraordinary. A profusion of loud and colourful parrots, such as Rainbow Lorikeets, brings a rich lustre to the Australian canvas. Just a few examples.

With these things in mind it is true to say that living in Australia presents the same joys, frustrations, anxieties, sorrows and unresolved dilemmas that exist for any people living anywhere. That is what is so wonderful about poetry. Down through the centuries and across all cultures, poetry so effectively encapsulates the cries for meaning, reconciliation, beauty and comfort that come from every human heart.

– Peter Stiles

Three
Postcards

1

last week they were pulling the house down next door.
smashing tiles, ripping timber from timber,
crushing the sightlines of more than thirty years.

now there is just a sunlit, fallow field.
by my dining room window, I wait, like a patient farmer,
for a new crop of redbrick memories to be planted in this place.

2

there is also the open space that my father used to fill,
his soft hands falling on the piano keys like
a careful conversation of love and gentleness.

in the breath between dusk and moonlight
I wait for those rippling fugues and sonatas,
the May frost settling on this clearing, this emptiness.

3

there's a hush on this bare field tonight,
as I pause for some good news from London.
another grandchild, a stella nova, to come into this void.

imperceptibly, brick by brick, note by note, smile by smile,
God turns back the barren fields of loneliness.
life is always a reaping and a replanting.

Long
Weekend
at Avoca

Early October, and the beach sings again
   with the voices of little children.
Springtime comes in Kandinsky colours
   splashed across each ultra violet day,
      like parakeets blinding the ear with their screeching.

My words are stayed in this heat.

For the moment, warmth of the skin,
   colour of youth, flick of water, a sandy limb,
      there is nothing to shape but contentment.

Waves, memories from childhood, wash in.

A young woman, fair, with Celtic fairness,
   photographs patterns traced by tides
      on the rock face beyond the beach.
She steps closer and closer, while others, oblivious,
   fish from the edge in their tanned silence.
Earnest, but peaceful, she reads the poems I cannot write,
   poems about deep time
      and the meaning of summers.

The
Beatitudes

On an early summer's day in Prague
   we step inside a gallery
      exhibiting the work of Alphonse Mucha.
Reluctant to leave the tourist-traipsed city square below
   our eyes take time, but then adjust to
      the delicate pastel tones and lines,
         walls of his detailed art nouveau.
Idealised, grace-filled female forms
   in patterned, symmetrical beauty,
      framed and arranged advertisements for
         Cycles Perfecta and *Théâtre de la Renaissance.*
A chronology of carefully crafted meal vouchers,
   selling a product to keep a man alive,
      creative flourishes shaped for daily bread.

It is cool and quiet in this place.

As we pass from one gallery space to another,
   forming our regard with comment and colour,
      a series of simple, rustic vignettes,
         'Blessed are' scenes with nothing to sell but their truth.

Even here, a displaced traveller,
   The words of Jesus slice through my reality:
Blessed are the merciful,
   Blessed are those who mourn,
      Blessed are the peacemakers.

Today, in the hush of solemnity,
    we visited the Jewish synagogues in Prague.
Killed with sneer and loathing
    the ordered names (just names) of thousands of
        children, men and women lined the walls of one.
Mucha himself, in 1939,
    died soon after being 'questioned' by the Gestapo.

Here, then, one fair city (for us, much awaited)
    displays both the zodiacs of love and hatred.

St Mary,
Star of the Sea,
Gerringong

it's star time of the year again,
December breezes cooling the steep climb.
our backs to the whitened church,
there is only silence now and the distant sea.

my gaze to the horizon is a prayer.

the star you placed within my sea of dreams
is the lingering brightness of a father's love.
there is a saintliness in parenthood
that Jesus knew, and draws me back to you.

be near, dear Lord, make all stars clear.

Poetry
Reading

Plates empty, door closed,
we listen along the lines of thought
    for sounds we know.
Pages open, a dozen paper owls
arc through the stillness of each mind
    for shaded corners.
We take turns in reading
and with each
the same swift winging.
Until,
someone reads a poem about his father
and owl feathers trapped in wire netting
    flurry in anguish.

A
Year
After
the
Bushfire

from within the blackness of last summer's fire,
grevilleas sprout and charred banksias bloom,
and, stooping and looking (intently, near)
I see God before me and witness his quilting,
a grand, reckless gesture of delicate miracles.

The
Concert

A Schumann sonata resonates
   in the cool air of the country hall,
      the violin singing
         mit leidenschaftlichem Ausdruck.

In the audience a young woman stirs.

Wide-eyed she sketches,
   her hand poised over
      the notepad in her lap.

Others glance at this listener
   who fashions images from sounds,
      deftly snaring quavers onto paper.

I look away
   and smile at the whimsy of writing a poem
      about someone drawing music.

Fruit
Picking

Quieter still we stand
and feel behind the apple's eye
the smeared warmth of sunshine humming.
Depthed in green
we pluck our pastels free,
but jolt at the roar of tractor
with a fresh load of cases.

Country
Town

town by a creek,
    creek-flat blurred by the morning mist.
childhood spent in a country town like this?
no Slessor gambols here, just the insistence of time,
    with willows whispering back over decades.
centennial park,
    brass cadences, and generations of lost words
        linger about the rotunda.
Constable tones, with a
    jade-like white draught horse by
        a stand of camphor laurels.
mid-morning,
the mist draws back to timbered hills.
a valley washed with pastures.
spaces of air and sun.
afternoon heat.
the barber lazes in his chair,
    fading Manchester,
        sweet smell of leather from the saddlery.
at dusk
    each worker shares a shadow with the evening sun.
an ebony pine,
    needled, and coneclustered
        against the darkening sky.
day files into the cool tomb of night.
night.
night is silence,
    until cats fight in a spangle of stars.

Waiting

A gentle room, I made it so
    with yellow chrysanthemums for you.
The refrigerator hums to itself,
    and timber shuffles in the ceiling.
By the radiator, a mawkish ceramic cat
    tears thoughts from the air.

I wait patiently,
    and watch fragmented clouds.

In the dolorous light
    rain traces down the gutters.
Wet leaves brush me,
    though against the glass,
        and a late bus stings the busy road,
            now bathed in streetlight.

Wind, like a nightwatchman
    moves around outside our house.

The telephone is silent.

Rainbow
Lorikeets

suburban Sunday.
that morning, lunch in the oven,
    I read it in the Herald.

torches trembling,
    archaeologists find ancient cave paintings
        in Wollomi National Park, so close to Sydney.
in a sacred moment,
tempo and space converge.

and, as with Saint Francis,
    wild birds gather in the treetops.
no fault line then in the world of men.

I waited.

the table was set, when,
    like a paint spill of blue, green and gold,
        lorikeets winged onto the back verandah;
the railing now a fiesta of cheerful sentinels.
with feigned annoyance,
I lunged at them to scatter.
reading my love,
    they rocked,
        then steadied themselves;
longing for me to plunge into their rainbow.

New
Year's
Eve,
2005

for David Brown

a humid December night in Sydney.
at a quarter to twelve,
surrounded by champagne glasses,
I read a poem by Wendell Berry.
soon, startling colours will
burst across the sparkling harbour.

this year, though,
    there is smoke in every hue,
        wormwood in every vintage,
            a rift in every resolution.
the pastor, friend, who loved these nights
    is gone, a melanoma seeding
        savagery throughout his body.

years ago it was a cooler night
    and we wrapped ourselves in blankets,
        like jocular monks
            strolling to evening vespers,
                posing for the photographs
                    I still have in my mind.

we laughed at life, for we were young,
    and the years spread out before us
        like boxes and boxes
            of carefully crafted sermons.

for four months
    we had prayed for him at every meal,
that kindness find a shelter from the pain,
    that grace keep goodness free
        a little longer.
but Berry's poem is true;
        the fault lines run so deep
            in this malignant world.

tonight across the light bathed harbour
    fun buds eternal in every youthful mind.
a new year is a new beginning, but,
    I cling on to my fashioned faith in love,
        a divine gesture that will rescue us
while leading down the flinty road he trod.

Anniversary

it is three years today since my father died,
but I still hear him whistling
      from room to room
the lines of that old Hoagy Carmichael tune
that he carried through life
      like a tonic
         from days
when his dance band was
      playing the nights into light
on cold weekends around Tenterfield.

For Derek

It was nearly Christmas and we stood
    on the balcony of your new Sydney home.
Before us stretched acres of close-cut lawns and
camphor laurels pleading for Mount Fuji coolness.
You spoke of your love for the Japanese language,
    the joy in a word, the trick of a phrase,
        your finger raised in
            a declaration of linguistic precision.
With each savoured nuance
      of these treasured cadences,
        you drew closer to a world
          of bamboo, silk and bonsai.
You raked over patterned sounds in your mind
      like pebbles in a neatly ordered garden.
You told me of your Japanese reading group,
      columns translated in joy from the newspaper.
Tilting backwards, with light in your eyes,
    laughter rippled from your face,
      like a haiku master
        pleased with the very best words.

Matilda's First Christmas

bushfires,
    in the Blue Mountains.
a city cloaked in smoke.
at dusk,
the sun is a coal-fire.

earlier, a baked dinner
(pork with crackling)
laughter and goodwill
    punctuating
the rush of wind
    against the house.

this morning, after church,
    we opened presents -
a fiesta of
    green and crimson paper
        beneath the Christmas tree.

some brightness is inside
    this Christmas,
her presence sweetening
    every smile.

last night,
    through open windows,
the stars blazed.

yesterday, we cut
    Christmas bush,
red, like a bush burning.
today,
    we let fire into our hearts.

a child is born.

Cutting
a Christmas
Tree

in the heat of summer
   and this profusion of pines,
      my son's eye rests
         on a single tree.

delighted by such grace,
   I measure out my life in Christmas trees.

Stigmata

(from a walking track in the
Blue Mountains on Good Friday)

someone is hammering nails into timber.

across the eucalyptic haze of distant hills
descending cadences of impact slice the silence,
as each nail reaches deep into the grain.
someone is fencing a block or putting down decking.

my thoughts in nearby fern-lined paths
are pierced by a pattern of migrainous throbs.
I see his hands on coarse hewn wood,
I feel his pain, my wrists in carpal tunnel agony.

Whitsunday
at Wentworth
Falls

a crisp winter evening settles on the Blue Mountains.
here are all the elements for peace.
silence,
    and a warming fire after a cloudless day.
outside, bowed gumtrees stand
    close to the house,
        like holidaymakers around a camp fire.
tonight,
    one match to the set kindling,
        and the flames rise hungrily
            to the split wood.
I have seen that fire before, that fire I know,
    that splintered hearts can be consumed by love
        and in the dark like radiant embers glow.

The
Flight
into Egypt

(from a Coptic Orthodox icon)

I set this small icon before me.
I will try to listen and not speak.
'Out of Egypt will I call my Son.'
The gold, embossed letters underscore
    an entry and a departure,
        a retreating from safety and
            a returning in readiness.
Even for you, Lord, there were times
    when the threat of sharpened hate
        meant the cover of obscurity.

But the golden haloes ring me in security,
    centuries of quiet triumph
        in their stylised circularity.
Mary cradles the infant close to her cheek.
Joseph looks upwards to the guiding angel.
This is a platter of gold and crafted richness,
    russet, autumnal tones with olive,
        burgundy, browns in careful balance.
The donkey has a saddle fitted for royalty,
    and its stare to the questioning viewer is
        more than dumb recognition.

The Egyptian landscape is replete
    with palms, wheat and bulrushes.
Fish feed as the donkey passes by,
    like followers wanting to catch
        the crumbs of His goodness.
Lilies festoon the shore beside the Nile.
The sky is a vaulted cavity,
    enclosing the travelling party
        in paternal shadow.
For this is a land of spare and ancient buildings,
    bleached and bare in the ruthless, heedless sun.

But false Ra has no power over Jesus,
    and Herod cannot make this child his prey.
This retinue will speak from age to ageless,
    in a voice of simple, coded confidence.
As I look at this small icon set before me,
    I will try to listen and not speak.
I will shape my thoughts around this tight-wrapped infant,
    and touch the hem of his regal saddlecloth.
This is a poem about listening, not speaking,
forget I ever wrote it, come and pray.

Easter
Saturday

late afternoon.
I am plodding through the briars
    of my consciousness,
equating memories, manuscripts and meanings,
Duruflé's *Agnus Dei* leavening my thoughts.

where are the margins of a father's love?
across the stark, cold surfaces of separation
it whispers still, like an autumn sough
in the blurred shadows outside my window.

it gently pleads for a renewing, a returning,
father and son together
    in the glow of a festive table,
their love basted with laughter and good wine,
displacing any void that surfaces as loneliness.

sometimes I walk with the father,
    sometimes with the son.
today I see a father's pain, in cruel focus,
cradling his bitterness, that the limitless sky
must contain this fracture, this rent perfection.

Dali's
Christ
on the
Cross

I look down like a father
    on your luxuriant head of burnished hair,
        so damp with anguish and despair.
Your arms stretched taut against the cross,
    pectoral muscles twisted and taut in final agony.
Your hands are frozen, rigid in trauma,
    raw, rough clouts driven through the palms,
        all tenderness stolen from your gentle touch.
Stifled, like drowning, your hands and ankles carry
    the full weight of your body.
From above, where I am, the afternoon light
    illuminates your earthly form and the cross
        lacquering it all with suggestive sunshine,
            suspending both against the black, vacuous sky.
This is a vertiginous perspective,
    I don't feel comfortable here.
Better for me to be kneeling beneath this cross,
    or, like a humble fisherman beside his boat,
        drawing in salty nets in simple acts beside a lake,
        awed and forever thankful
            for the magnitude of this offering.

Grace

I am trumped by grace, mocked by love,
forced to look to God above.
busy in my mannered schemes
your goodness shines
through plans and dreams
of polished cars and fresh-turned page
emails, sorting, and dry, raked leaves.
in stillness I hear your gentle voice,
nuanced and fine, definition defied,
the palate, the colour of premium wine.
Lord Jesus, even French oak casks,
are unworthy of this vintage, vast,
firm in its character, quietly poured
into the heart by a loving Lord.
your voice brings me back to a wooden cross
without you all my days are loss.

The Visitation

I remember them well.
Moments that were
    meant for metaphors,
        the lightning brightness
        of his visitation.
No words matched the
    thrown open shutters
        of his festive presence.
More than angling sunshine
    through a bedroom window,
Or sky wide evening embers
    in this winter valley.
Like a Lutheran steeple that
    snatched my breathing,
        surprising my laughter
        with its burnished brilliance.

Separation

there has always been silence
   when there should have been words.
      a mother smiling, waving,
         from a hospital ward window
            to a pale boy, hair combed,
               peering from the street below.
                  her separation from him unexplained,
                     this is no remedy for pain.

there has always been silence
   when there should have been words.
      a mother, father, staring,
         from the honeysuckle-filled verandah,
            captured in the sepia tones
               of a young man's college camera.
                  their feelings never spoken,
                     eyes skating far from bonds now broken.

there has always been silence
    when there should have been words.
        a gaunt mother, adhering to life
            like a feather to a windscreen,
                never saying time, goodbye,
                    the dark thoughts never mentioned.
                        this is no remedy from pain,
                            no briared words when final moments came.

there has always been silence
    when there should have been words.
        a father, whistling, joking to the last,
            no words to say that it is done.
                when we were wedding guests his life
                    climbed quickly to the sun.
                        intended as a silent remedy from pain,
                            those words unspoken make my speaking plain.

Breakfast in Assisi

for Matilda

The Assisi air was clear
  as a pilgrim's bell that morning.
We climbed the steep road
  to the Basilica in nourished silence,
    the stillness like warm bread taken
      straight from the baker's oven.

Three Capuchins sat on a nearby wall,
  dancing their eyes by the place
    where he had been,
      where he saw poverty and broken
        bread as a wholesome breakfast.

Later we laughed at the thought
  that they might be cappuccinos,
    which you said you always like
      with a chocolate croissant
        in Primrose Hill.

Come, Holy Spirit

Come, Holy Spirit, touch my eyes,
  that I might fall in darkness at His feet,
    and then with clearer vision later rise.

Come, Holy Spirit, break my heart,
  it never yet has loved Him as it should,
    remake it with the drumbeat of His art.

Come, Holy Spirit, guide my hands,
  that they may touch the cup of living wine,
    and sense eternal springs in desert sands.

Come, Holy Spirit, take my days,
  that He might give me more to see the Cross,
    and mercy to repair my broken ways.

Come, Holy Spirit, use my voice,
  that it may sing in clear tones of His love,
    so wood and stone may resonate, rejoice.

Haiku

on colourless days
a steady lamp still burns within,
warming the tissue of love

Psalm 18:28

if I reach in through
the window of my childhood
the bed is still warm

if not in the wind
then this panoply of swirling leaves
tells me you are near

1 Kings 19:11

eagles inhabit North American poems
and sometimes alight in fierce proximity
to country roads near Sydney

For Margaret

the red kimono
passes, his steady eye on
a finer text of love.

For Uncle Innes

In
the
Garden

*'my soul is overwhelmed with
sorrow to the point of death'
(Matthew 26:38)*

outdoors, but seizing at air,
he fell,
        with his face to the ground.
shards of pain like slivered glass
            swallowed
                in his heart.
the garden was a shock of silence;
an infinity of love
            menaced by spears and clubs.

Reading
Seamus
Heaney

New reading glasses.
Left eye cloudy, as from birth,
    the right eye twenty, so that is plenty.
With cool rims resting on the bridge
    and tortoiseshell case snapped shut,
I scan these lines of framed memory,
    honing my thoughts as if behind your lenses,
        a Conway Stewart poised between my fingers.
You focus on a father digging
    flowerbeds in the morning light.
This lingering spectacle of an Irish childhood
    clarifies my horn rimmed sight.
I write.

I write of a boy in a country town
    his earliest years in myopic blur.
At five, his older brother died, parents pianissimo crying.
Detached from the retinue of muffled mourners,
    with pillow and blanket in the room next door
        he saw he could not.
Nor could he see them wearily digging
    the granite belt unmarked grave,
        poverty stinging his father's New England eyes.
Every year, from then, this boy watched his father digging
    flowerbeds into a summer metaphor,
        lenses wiped clear for such crystalline insight.

I now read and write by incandescent light.

Denniston,
New Zealand

Drive up from Westport into another world.
    Leaving the coastal plains you climb
        a darkly wooded mountain range,
           cloaked in mist and rain.
This is an ascension into sadness.
    The mine site and town are deserted now,
        neat heritage displays set amidst
           the rusting machinery
              and broken stone foundations.

Here are the photos of miners and their families.
    On this mountain top their lives were hewn,
        struck out of hardship,
           wept into love and memories.
Men stand wasted at the pithead,
    women dance the hard years away,
      children play on the flinty schoolyard.
The light in their eyes and tender hopes
    are swallowed by mist
        and the jeopardy of time.

Resurrection Sunday

A glorious unveiling, lightning, presence,
    a tearing, releasing, breathless running.
News that exploded like soul searing fission,
    for Jerusalem, Empire, Age, a tired Earth.
But a touching, a healing, a balm like no other,
    the bunting of grace in the shards of cruelty,
      the banner of joy for the grimace of sadness.

The
Creative
Impulse

The moment between the brush and canvas,
pen and paper,
hands and the keyboard,
the liminal space of uncertainty,
of unrevealed colours,
cadences and chords.
Looking inward to look outwards,
backwards to look forwards,
shaping.
In this moment the rush of concepts,
the blurring of possibilities,
the richness of choice.
A catching,
a directing,
a movement towards birthing,
A glimpsed outline,
the fragment of a story,
a recurrent modulation.
This is a moment to savour,
the wisp of otherness,
a gasp on the trapeze.

Winter
in the
Blue
Mountains

Ahead of the snow a disconnect,
   the moment between sunshine and darkening wind gusts.
Clearly something is missing;
   a space in the air,
      a space in the heart,
         the longing for presence.
Yesterday, in illumined stillness,
   we worked in the garden for hours.
Today, in an old café, décor tired,
   we could hear uncertainty in holiday voices,
      the window frames rattling against the sense of change.
Give to me what is coming, Lord,
   I cannot stay in this place between.
I need you close, so close, so real,
   like vermilion embers in the woodstove before me,
      shielding me from the clutch of cold.

Praise

Deep in a sea of golden staves,
    tincture of sun on a summer sky.
Strangely blunted distant sounds,
    and a whisper of thanks
      met with peace and gladness.
Why come to me for so little, Lord?
  A sheaf of grace
    for the husk of my scribbling,
Wheatfields of love
    for this kernel of praise.

Sunset
over
Little
Kaiteriteri

Just for a minute I sense perfection.
A summer's evening, still, cool, pensive,
    full moon lacquering the darkening water
        like an unfurled banner of gold.

Christchurch

Christchurch looks like a city recovering from the Blitz, a patchwork effect right across the central business district. Here a building clad in scaffolding, damage apparent beneath it; there a precious building front supported by a stack of shipping containers; and just around the corner a clear field, with only a photographic memory of what once came into view. Some sacred spaces are like Roman ruins, the Cathedral of the Blessed Sacrament, once solid and dominant, now wounded and terminal, almost too painful to observe. A bleeding bastion, with too recent recollections. Where the CTV building collapsed is just an empty block greened over, easier to avert eyes and minds from that excessive pain.

Christchurch Cathedral. Images are everywhere. A postcard of the Rose Window, a carefully crafted wooden replica, a published history of the city includes various perspectives. It inhabits the mind of those in the South Island, but the reality no longer matches the sacred space that we would like to exist. It eludes sentimentality because it is so painful. Something that we believed in and was beautiful has been torn apart. It only lives in the mind now and in scattered images.

But hope buds everywhere as well, and humour too. Shipping containers of many colours, red, blue, green, are converted into boutique shops, the smallest units of safety possible. A bookstore, a coffee shop, exclusive labels, all sold from cosy containers that defy the vulnerability of this 'jelly city' (as one wry shop owner names it). A flower festival in the main square, an irony of colour sprouting from the stubble of the city's heart, the irresistible hope of human endeavour. Saint Michael and All Angels, with matai timber ceiling and pews, dark, aromatic, still and serene, stands like a spiritual jewel at the centre of the city. Virtually unscathed, it is a reminder of the indiscriminate nature of earthquakes, of life. It is also an emblem of the beauty that can come again.

Late Winter

Today is trying to be Spring,
  with hat blown back
    and sunshine in her face.

New
Black
Shoes

The end of another week of footfalls
and the evening sun seeps
in through my bedroom windows.
I take off my Burberry tie and shoes.
Constantly polished,
these old black shoes scuff my memory.
How many times have I tied their laces
and walked the halls
to dinners, interviews and meetings.
They mark a calendar of formality,
the pleasant tread of past commitments.

Spreadeagled on my bed I think about the future.

In the corner is a shoe box
with new black shoes
wrapped in crisp, white paper.
I bought them over a week ago.
I have lifted the lid a few times
to inhale the strident sweetness of new leather
to examine their pristine, parade gloss finish.

They are like a promise that the new has come,
that tomorrow I'll be striding down the street.

Excelsis Deo

Warm September,
   my window open to the clear night sky.
Someone has pinpricked the darkness with light.
The melody I pen
     from left to right
        lifts off the page
           in notes of praise
and scatters quavers through the trees.
Startled currawongs sing their part,
   picking up the new song in my heart.

The
Dead
Jacaranda

The night before the chain saw pieced
  my brittle, stark, skeletal friend,
    I took a small sprig from its fork.
It had been clutching there for years,
  pushing its way into a meagre existence
    of two and then three, four, five leaves.
I potted it carefully against the future,
  to remind me of this jacaranda tree
    whose lilac blossoms, each November,
festooned some of the best years of my life.

The
Crab Apple
Tree

We stood beneath the flowering crab apple,
    the pink and white blossom
        like clusters of cream and strawberry icing
            sprayed throughout the slender branches.
Plentifully sprinkled with frenzied honeybees
    the old tree, backlit by the morning sun,
        triumphantly glistened –
           a dessert prepared for Springtime.

For
C. S. Lewis

Lewis loved the Malvern Hills.
From their green spine the shires
    spread like a brushstroke before him.
I have the photos,
    and Elgar alludes to the delighting music
        of their summer evenings.

But, as with Narnia, I have never been there.

Trusting their reality, I press on,
    sharing his taste for the more
        tangible delights of marmalade and tea.

The
Kilns

For C.S.Lewis

I have been here before.
From the moment we parked outside, I knew it.
There is Jack, out in the morning light,
   greeting the gardener, Fred, his 'indispensible factotum',
      his deep voice donning the streets of Headington.
The air is still, with August warmth,
   the path to the front door crested with climbing roses.
The latch lifts.
From inside, through a familiar window,
   Jack and Joy still lean against that garden wall.
The blackout curtains are there yet,
   a reminder of dark nights, and lightless train trips to London,
      steaming through, like pot after pot of steeped ideas,
         ready for those famous BBC radio talks.
This is the desk he works at. Touch it.
 In sepia tones he sits there,
   paper, pen, Quink ink, tin of tobacco, pipe,
      crafting Christological concepts,
         answering a shuffle of letters with equal care.
In the shadows a household of voices,
   Warnie, Minto, evacuee Jill,
      attendant tones through the tangle of years.
Outside, I tip my hat to the cat before
   back down the streets he knows we head,
      into the bustling mind of Oxford.

The
Death
of John
Lennon

Night.
Across the lake a galaxy of streetlights.
Occasionally bright headlights flash,
    a supernova.
Like one man dying in a blaze of brilliance.

The
Three
Altar
Windows

St. Mary's Church, Gosford

Two men work in the lower windows
  on either side of the regal, shepherd Christ.
In vestments of red and gold he holds
  a cradled lamb in one arm, a crook in the other.
A complex of celestial portals looms above him.
This is the customary ambiguity
  of Earth and Heaven.

Not so for the men, though.
One is a young sower,
  a full bag of seed on his aching shoulder.
The other an aging fisherman,
  laden fishing net hauled by the lake.
Familiar, but for the clothes they wear,
Broad-brimmed felt hat, neckerchief,
  trousers turned up for colonial labour,
    the garments tear at
      our comfortable categories.

So far from Galilee, so far from Westminster,
These two men are doubly removed for a lifetime.
The sower becomes the fisherman
  in a land where stylized lilac clouds in an azure sky
    are like bluebells in a paddock under gum trees.
But, antipodean incongruities
  have become our way of life,
    and Christ's love like a brilliant paint spill
      over time and place.

Bread

We are opening Luke's Gospel after breakfast,
  a broken loaf of wholemeal bread
    before us on the kitchen table.
Filtered sunlight caught the morning scene
  in gumleaf shadows,
    like some Rembrandt memory.

The stillness was basted by October winds
  from the nearby valley.
You read the words of Jesus
  carefully, clearly, as always.

Sometimes, lost in a timeless dream of longing,
  I can but take this bread,
    touch and break its wholesome reality,
      smell the warmth of the bakery oven,
        and believe.

Thankfully, every morning there is bread.

Matilda's
Magic

Opening a packet of sparkle
  on the Persian hearth rug,
    my granddaughter, singing,
      spread a galaxy of stars
        across the welcoming surface.

Later that day,
  we prudently vacuumed up
    this act of cosmic excitement.

Tonight, by the fire, as I write this poem,
  many months have passed.
But, even now, in the silence,
  one green star still winks at me.

For
John

Sipping tea, we pass thoughts like Venetian glass.
I, blushing, tell of poems unspawned, and
  you, of Arctic wastelands where
    steel collides with ice,
      fine filaments of light
        shattering the silence.
You, gentle man, design an ice breaker?
Your Scottish lilt wistfully tells of
  engineering skill against white eternity.
My mind sweats in the afternoon warmth.
I proffer phrases like
  'What special qualities are?' and
    you continue to fill my glass, adding ice cubes.
A red ship on the slips,
  bulk awesome, bow like a polished blade.
My poems dissolve before your blueprint.
You, gentle man, design an ice breaker?
In the garden our children
  crack croquet mallets against coloured balls.

The
Country
School

As I stand under speechless gums,
   tank-traps around my country school,
      this outpost,
         a misfit in a land of green and brown,
            keeps quoting Vance Packard at me.

However,
   as I pause on a nearby hill,
      the burning roof of midday sun consumes
         snap-tab,
            glad-wrap,
               mad-cap man ideas,
      refines God, and
         pours Him over the countryside.

Postscript

God
in rainwarm nights
thrown
like a cape over the daydazed
I am hemming my loves with words
and dreams.

Acknowledgements

Grateful acknowledgement is made to the editors of the following publications, in which some of the poems first appeared:

The Regent Anthology, 'Poetry: Art Translated from Life', Summer Session, 1987, Regent College, Vancouver: 'Poetry Reading' and 'For John'

Christianity and Literature (2001, 2004): 'St. Mary, Star of the Sea, Gerringong', 'A Year after the Bushfire', 'Haiku', Postscript'

Studio (2007): 'Stigmata'

The Christian Teachers Journal (2008): 'The Flight into Egypt'

Set Free (Poetica Christi Press, 2004): 'Whitsunday at Wentworth Falls', 'Come, Holy Spirit'

My Brother, My Sister, My Country (Poetica Christi Press, 2006): 'Rainbow Lorikeets', 'Country Town'

Earth Works (Poetica Christi Press, 2007): 'Long Weekend at Avoca'

New Beginnings (Poetica Christi Press, 2010): 'Three Postcards', 'New Black Shoes'

Everyday Splendour (Poetica Christi Press, 2011): 'Matilda's Magic'

'Stigmata' and 'Long Weekend at Avoca' were also included in *Stonework*, the online literary journal of Houghton College, New York, 2006

'Three Postcards' was also displayed in The Christ Church Contemporary Art Space, Gosford, NSW as part of 'An Exhibition of Postcard Artworks', 2007. In addition, it was exhibited at the Al-Kahf

Gallery, Bethlehem, 2008, and the Regional Centre for Educational Planning, Sharjah University City, Sharjah, United Arab Emirates, 2008

Quadrant (November, 2015): 'The Beatitudes'. A version was also read and displayed at the Sesquicentenary celebrations of St. Mary's Heritage Church, Gosford, NSW, 2008

(spaces) (The Literary Journal of Trinity Western University, 2013-2014): 'Waiting'

'Fruit Picking' won the Armidale Teachers' College Poetry Prize in 1964

The Mundane Egg, Volume 1, 1973: 'The Country School'

OTHER BOOKS FROM POETICA CHRISTI PRESS

If you like this book, you might like some of these other poetry
anthologies published by Poetica Christi Press. To order, go to:
www.poeticachristi.org.au

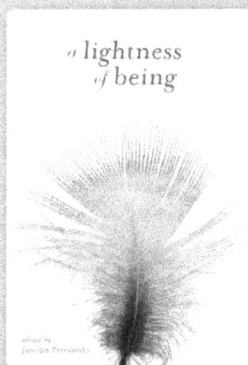

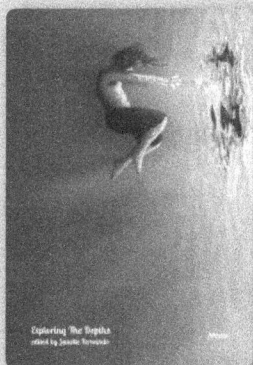

Poetica Christi Press
'Proudly publishing Australian poetry for 25 years'

www.ingramcontent.com/pod-product-compliance
Lightning Source LLC
Chambersburg PA
CBHW030154070426
42447CB00032B/1193